Then My Mind Took a Walk to Love

by

Cathy Aman
"Oakley"

ISBN: 0-75962-619-7

This book is printed on acid free paper.

1stBooks – rev. 10/31/01

Dedication

*This book is dedicated to my grandparents John and
Naomi Aman whose lives reflected poetry in motion to me.
To my daughter Megan whose joy renews me.
To my deceased mother Dorothy A. Aman who loved making
friends, was a fun and interesting mother and my best supporter
as an adult.
To the Klebes, my mother's parents Alvro and Vela and the many
aunts and uncles and cousins for their varied elements of humor,
spice and surprise.
To my father Rolland G. Aman whose philosophical
view of life has romanced me through some of life's difficulties.
And to all of the friends, teachers and acquaintances who have
touched my life deeply enough to inspire me to write.*

*I would like to give recognition and special thanks to Jim Groth
who gifted me with the cover photo, Kurt Tarkiainen who
contributed the photo for "Great Bay", my sister and brother-in-
law, Sue and Gary Clynick for contributing the "Couple In
Darkness" photo.*

POETRY TABLE OF CONTENTS

Happy

ANNIVERSARY

On this occasion
it is clear
that all your children
should be near.

So it is with grief
and deep despair,
that I
cannot be there.

As all have come
from far and near
to celebrate
this 50th year.

Of many smiles
and many tears
that you shared
throughout the years.

In greatest love
you've come through
I feel so glad
and proud of you.

Now I wish you blessings
from above
and sent to you
my deepest love.

New York City
July 1978
Aman Grandparents 50th

ANTSAFA*

I saw the parted lovers
fall like silent snow.
In frozen crystals
now upon the pavement.

Their love scattered,
a dispersed white confetti;
quietly descending
but with a voice
as loud as thunder.

Love now parted
in stillness lies waiting.
Preparing for spring
a morning, a new sky,
a warm love again to bring.

> Waltham, MA.
> December 7, 1992
> For Terrick

*Antsafa-the term for "inquires about things of which one is fully cognizant before hand."

Cathy Aman

ASIA RESTAURANT

Oh Asia,
stagnant air
a layer of frying grease
across my face
I breath your stale
clouds of smoky air.

I looked out across
your red décor
the taste of tobacco
at the back of my throat
Table 22, the one for eight
sits threateningly empty,

        Dover, NH
        while working at
        the Asia Restaurant
        late with a headache

BIRTH OF A FLOWER

In this little garden bright
an egg sleeps by candle light.
Tanned shell cracked a new,
glistening in morning dew.

Velvet peddles fall aside
as awakes the rose deep inside.
Red rose stands behind my back
in front a contrast to wearing black.

Cords of life, purple, blue and gold
with a lovely stem that I can hold.
Now a vase to put her in,
sit back and let the show begin!

A satin jacket to wear at night
with a large gold button to catch the light.
Knotted belt with a satin hook
adds a comfortable bounteous look.

Change now from black to emerald green
leaves you looking rather like a queen.
If you mix and match these as you please,
you'll find varied fashion is a breeze.

Now from green to peaches and cream,
or plush brown velvet is quite a dream.
My first coat looks a bit like an eastern sky.
Cotton spring blouses were my next try.

Cathy Aman

Coming are textured fabrics of royal hue.
These too come to mind as I think of you.
These were stitched by hand in wintry nights
so, in rememberence of snow, I've made some whites.

Now in sharing my hearts delight,
is a friend to take pictures as I write.
We pray to stand in God's glorious light
as we share the celebration of your wedding night.

Waltham, MA
December 1992
Grandparents 65th

BONDAGE

There are memories
    sleeping in our clocks
        waiting for time to pass,
        waiting to awake.

These are hearts
    in our garages
        pounding hard because they are cold,
        longing for warm hands to touch them.

There is love
    in our minds
        hiding behind brains afraid to feel,
        hoping to be found.

                Jacksonville, Ill.
                August 18, 1971

BRANCH

Little branch, with wood brown
as a chestnut.
Fine thorns piercing
outward like headless
pins.

Berries dried
yet clinging
hang heavy
and red as
blood.

Durham, NH
April, 1982

CARLA'S BIRTHDAY

So soft so soft
　　it wanted to float away.

Her hair across her pillow lay
　　but hearing the music it decided to stay.

Whispering winds
　　blew right through her mind.

Leaving the fading music behind
　　aware of what waited, of what she may find.

May 8, 1981
Carla's Birthday

CAROUSEL

A carousel, a carousel
Horses of yellow, horses of blue
galloping to music.
I've painted a carousel of color for you.

Horses of brown
dappled and blue.
A carousel of horses
are waiting for you.

Manes fly in the wind
they gallop in time
to music boxed verses
this carousel of mine.

CIRCLES OF LIFE

River, oh river that runs to the sea
Ocean with waves that clasp and lie upon the land.
Land rolls onto mountains,
Mountains reach to sky.
Sky expands above to embrace the clouds
Clouds weep and wail…
Lie your tears upon the sand.
And tears fall onto land again,
To make rivers that run to the sea,
To make rivers that run to the sea.

The circles of nature
The circles of life
Spinning around us creating the force of our lives.
The Universe powered by minus and plus,
pulling the forces around us.
The stars and the moon, lakes and trees,
reaching the warm land that lies by the sea.
Winter that passes and melts with the rain.
The birds fly north again.
The birds fly north again.

Spinning cocoon of fine silk threads,
butterfly inside but never dead.
Worm that ate the green green leaves
now inside the silken sleeve.
New life between these emerald walls.
Butterfly born when nature calls.
Dance on the breeze
from flowers with pollen
on through the trees.
Basking in sun she relieves.

Goldsmith makes a lovely fine ring
that lies on the hand of a king.
The king has died and treasures pass
across the sea at last.
The boat in a storm is met by waves
by pirates their sailors taken as slaves.
Treasure is lost at the center of sea.
Gold ring is lying…
Now it comes to the beach to me.
Treasures in sand that fall to the shore,
Gifts from the sea and more.
Yes, diamonds and gold within the sea untold.

Hammer and nail meet the hard wood.
The man builds a house as he know he should,
house that stands in the prairie near woods,
stands as an island alone.
'mungst the woods the house meets fire
and turns to ashen stone.
Goes to the soil to make it rich,
so another tree there can grow.
Grow in its place, branching fine lace
and talk of the stalk to the leaves.
Mighty oaks that dance in the breeze.

Durham NH
November 1980

Cathy Aman

CITY TEARS

Let me go back
     go back
     into the city to cry my tears.

Where city sounds
     absorb the wailing
     to hide deep in the forest of city.

               New York City
               Children's Day
               October 28, 1981

COLD EYES

A frozen face
hung over an old coat slouched in disappointment.

It was a cold day,
the clouds a steely kind of gray.

One cloud burst.
Open faced he received the drifting flakes.

Large flakes,
floated down like laced confetti.

Silent descending stars
melted into the warm pools of his sad eyes.

Icy beads cooled his tears
he opened his mouth and began to laugh.

Cathy Aman

COUPLE IN DARKNESS

We were thinking of things pure,
side by side, along the paths.
We were holding hands.
Without speaking…among the dark flowers,

we strolled like a couple betrothed,
alone, in the green night of the fields,
sharing fruits of the land
under a moon friendly to madness.

Then without words we lay dead,
on the moss, far away,.
all alone, in the soft shadows
of the intimate murmuring woods.

Above us, in the immense light,
we found ourselves weeping.
We had arrived in love
my dear companion of silence!

DANCER

I am a dancer in my mind,
    don't you know?
I am a dancer!

I am dancing high
    far above the world,
lighter than a cloud.

My hands reach out.
    Planted firmly on the earth,
I embrace it and set it free!

Melodies move my mind.
    Each beat strikes a chord
sending vibrations to my soul.

Dance my soul!
    Whirl and bound. Set me free!
For I am a dancer and I set still.

Durham, NH
April 25, 1980
Listening to piano music with
bad headache

Cathy Aman

DANCING TREES

Dancing trees close their eyes
      to the chanting moon.
Blue winds
      blow horror through the valleys.

A fat man sat in the corner
      and you prayed
you'd stay in this
      plain of time forever.

Too frightened to close
      your eyes. Too tired
to hold them opened.
      Too curious to lie empty.

Untouched
      Unseen
But present

      South Dakota
      1970's

DEAR 60'S

You came like a dream,
but you are a memory.
I am too willing to forget
the sorrows you brought me.
Like a blade you lanced the nations wound
letting the blood of unspoken thoughts,
of dreams repressed.

But you lanced with an unclean blade,
letting infection fester inside.
As with syphilis, our nation was blinded.
Open conflict across her face.
My mind cries for revolution.
My ears ache to hear life's music.
My soul desires to love.

The fibers of life set ablaze
in search of new life.
But burned to ash
when no answer came
even within themselves.
How may ash be reconstructed?
So many left lying,
hardly distinguishable
from dust…

Durham, NH
September 1980

DREAMER

In the stillness of the day
he rest his weary head,
right there on natures lap
he did proceed to nap.

"Sweet lullaby I hear," he said
"from birds there in the trees
musically swaying grasses
played by breezes as they pass."

While snuggled in earth's bosom
he gazed into yonder blue.
The clouds began to dance
changing form at every glance.

His eyelids kissed
and dreams were born
meeting streets of another world.
There his imagination was unfurled.

Something wet and trickling in his eyes
broke that wondrous sleep.
And waking quickly there to find
dark clouds before the sun that shined.

Now lazy dreamer to your feet!
The sun is low.
The time has passed and you are late.
Alas, the lazy dreamers late.

Durham , NH
Summer 1980

DYING ROSE

A dying rose
      hung its
            `head,
      shedding petals
like over sized tears.

A dry thorn
      pierced my flesh.
            Blood gathered
      in a small bead,
red as a new blossom.

                        Boston, MA

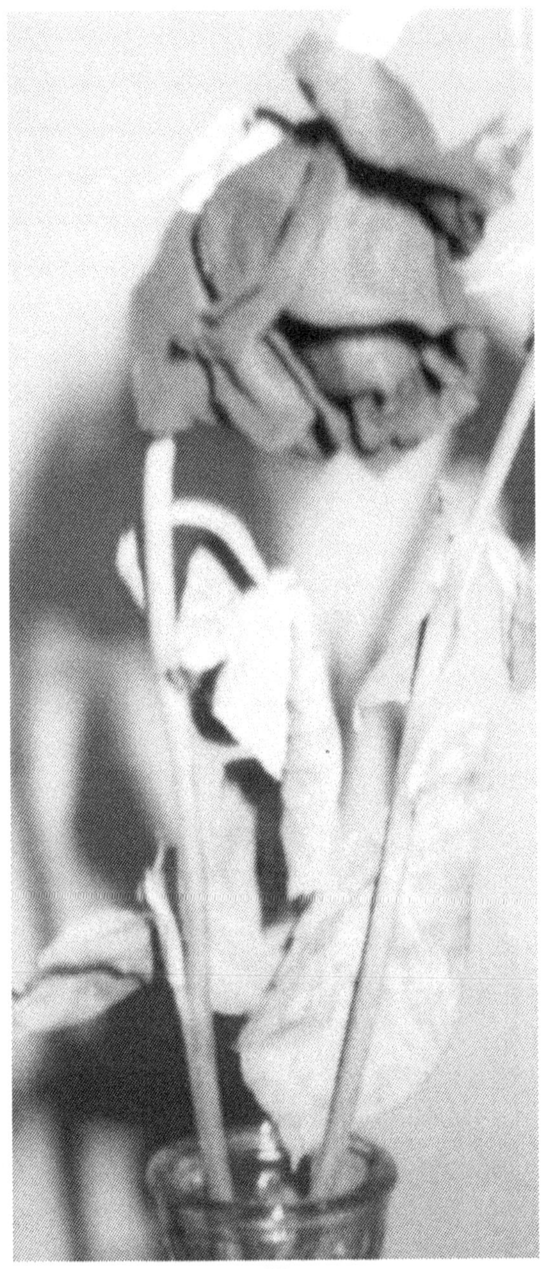

EGG

Cast in shadow,
cast in white;
unglazed
you hold your secret within.

You sit
so anonymously.
No face, no front
no back.

Had you a voice
would you cry
that what is within
will never be born?

Or are you as you appear?
Dulled apathetic
barely able to
reflect light?

Thin
frail
and simply
a shell.

New Hampshire 1980's

Cathy Aman

EMERGENCE

I'm in love with men
      who dream,
minds riding on the surf of night.
      Men of patience,
of loyal heart.
    They lift the world
in courage to proclaim
   what goes beyond
the confidence of eyes.
   Climatic call,
then descend to the pit of the earth
   with birds now rise to a higher note.

New Hampshire 1980's

FOLLOW YOUR HEART

Follow your heart
that richest pearliest part of you.

Where you are pure
and solid as tempered gold.
Where things are not dry or hard
but as reaching down to lush spring mosses
Where your joyful tears and gratitude
blend humbly to an abundant heart.
There you are…

That is the real you.
Princes and princesses, lords of the earth.
Of lofty trees that always seem to reach out
out stretching their limbs to the true you.
Lords of the cattle and all creatures,
of the oceans which pound their mammoth beat
Embracing the beaches
cradling the land.

Follow that heart
which has long lain hidden and silent within
It is you
and it is a treasure
Be the treasure that you are.

FOREST WATCH

A forest of children
      time turns
A deer lies hidden
      in summer grasses
He is quiet to maintain
      his secret
The edge of night skies
      lingers on
Waiting for dawn
      to break
Waiting for day to fill
      its place

Aberdeen, SD
October 26, 1971

GARDEN OF LIFE

Let me be the seed in your garden,
that I may be nourished in the rich soil
of your knowledge.

That your experienced hand
may pry the weeds whose
roots lie deep and hidden
sucking life elements from within.

That my mind may come to
blossom fragrant in thought,
my life bear the fruit of
victory for mankind,
my seed to proclaim the glory
of true parents.

Durham NH
1980's to Tiger Park

36

GOD

I know you are there
        a sky watching over us.
As a brimming moon
        guide us through long darkness.
How we long for you
        for those who would know your heart.
You, the jewel
        that out shines the Northern Star.
Autumn odors fill the air
        rising from a leaf bedded soil
You penetrate our hearts
        with an untouchable warmth
Your truth crystallizes our thought
        as a new day turns evening snow to diamonds.

GREAT BAY

I plunged into the
cold waters of the
Great Bay.
My eyes cracked like ice
and I began to see.

Beneath the stone ledge
is a garden
with flowers
like I have
never seen.

Trees with bows
that shoot skyward
as fountains.
Weeping willows that
wrap me in tresses wet with tears.

GREY HOUND GOOD-BYE

And I leave you behind
           old city…
               torn hearts.

How you have striven,
           toiling flows
               through your veins.

But what were you building?
           What was your dream?
           What lies ahead?

It must be more than
           just another day.
               My heart tears.

Dry your eyes.
           We won't part again.
           My arms won't close to you.

                   Minneapolis,MN.
                   February 1980

42

I WENT HOME

I went home.
   I walked the fields,
      drank from the spirit of the earth,

From a hawk
   a deer,
      and a butterfly

From the spirit of
   an open field of wheat
      and one of blooming purple clover.

The wind sang to me.
   The muffled thunder of horse hooves
      on plowed land stirred my soul.

I went home and was awakened
   to life, to love
      to God. I am alive.

I walk carrying a jewel within.
   Each step is conscious, knowing the value
      of my content.

        It's name
        Christ Love

                South Dakota

Cathy Aman

IN THE GARDEN

Well don't you know in the garden
what your life could have been?

You fell in the garden
far from my highest dream

You left me in the garden
standing all alone

With you gone from the garden
it made a prison of my home

Come back to the garden
though with weeds now over grown

For you and I in the garden
is our hearts only home

Come back to the garden
I need you. I'm all alone

I watched from the garden
as your feet dipped to the mud

And I cried in the garden
seeing the land splattered with your blood

Rain fell near the garden
you drowned in your own tears

Come back to the garden
let's share our remaining years

Come back to the garden
there we'll live for 10,000 years

Forever then in the garden
forever in your heart

I'll be the tender of the garden
from there our Heaven will start

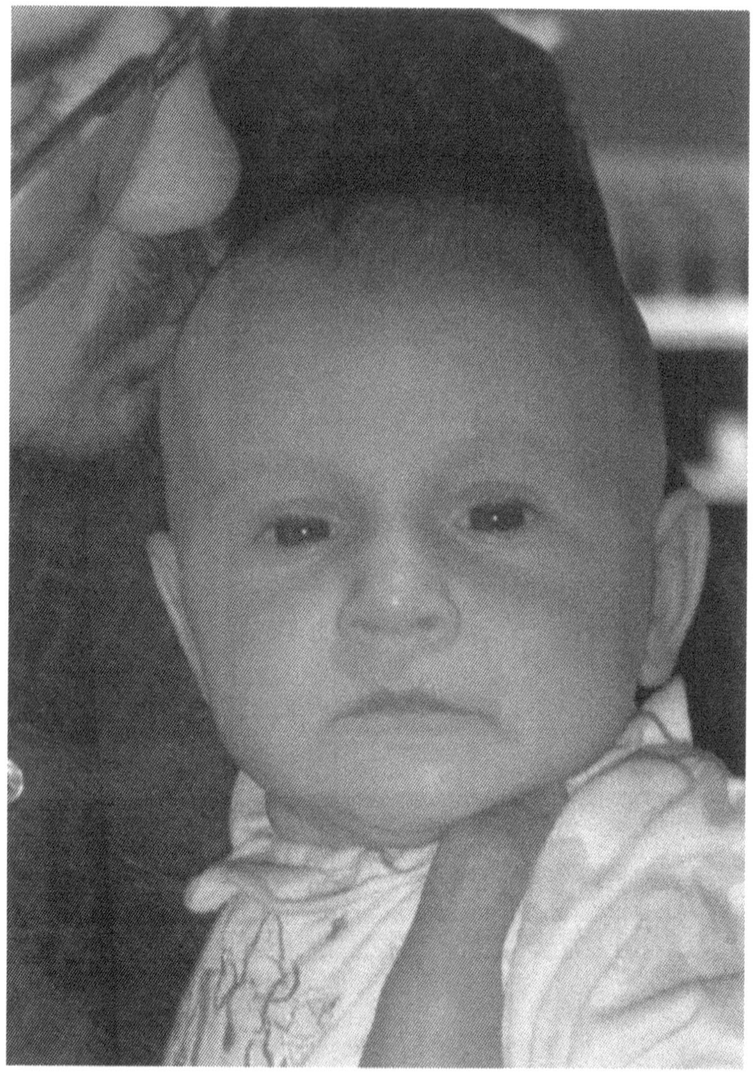

INTO EYES

Your love blows
through my soul
and I became light.
My bones become
like hollow reeds
moaning a sweet and melancholy tune.

I look into your eyes
They look back
like two dark tunnels
calling and inviting me
to enter and explore.

Cathy Aman

IT DEPENDS

I waited and waited.
Life ticks by
like an impatient
clock that won't
stop to give you the time of day.

Waddle and wade
in mud that oozes
just above your knees.
It's enough to hold you down
unless you wanted to step out.

Make up your mind
based on a cloud
that changes it's form
in the next gust of wind.
Focus on a cloud
but the sky is still the same.

Did you think this life was yours
to have to hold
like a handbag which you change
with each new mood,
in which you carry
only what you wish?

Durham,NH
May 3, 1980

KITE

A mountain in the cold of night.
A mountain top to fly a kite.
A hillside grassed green and fine.
The time is theirs. The life is mine.

To gaze upon her curves and slopes,
fills my mind with joyous hopes.
If we climb we'll soon be there,
to let gentle breezes toss our hair.

> Aberdeen, SD.
> April 17, 1971

Cathy Aman

LONELINESS

Loneliness you come,
and like a bird,
descend quietly from behind.
Your delicate feet
pad tenderly upon my shoulder.
I give a silent nod
to acknowledge your presence
you blink…

There is a gust of wind
and I am
in flight.
Holding close
to your body
as we glide through
gray and rippled
winter sky.

You carry me
from the
earth's surface.
Trees become twigs.
Roof tops like
the patterned
squares of a
patch work quilt.

I snuggled close
and feel
the throbs of
your small heart.
Your body is warm,
feathers ruffle
folding softly about
my chilled flesh.

In childish wonder
I would ask
our destination
but know
in silent
unspoken words,
that I have already
been told.

Who'd have thought
these hollow bones
fragile as twigs
could take us
to such heights?
I look before us, my hair
combed back by
cooled fingers of the wind.

Clouds bow down
their doors.
They greet us
with humus nature,
then adorn us
with clear and sparkling
beads of jeweled
evening dew.

Cathy Aman

Continuing in white
as if through
winters canyon.
Dissolving visions
of past and future.
Flight.
through the staccatoed
tune of NOW .

Heavens gold finger
dips into the river
of white. Lifting us
above this moody dune.
Now revealing
as a hidden treasure
the golden splendor
of a sunlit sky.

LONGING FOR INDIA

My friend is like a river
of which I've never seen the source.

Flowing down from a high place
he runs deep with clear thoughts.

Thoughts reflective of daylight
run musically over cool stones of longing.

Waves ripple musically over images of the past.
The river expands. Its destiny vanishes

beyond my sight.
But its course is set to the sea.

Dover, NH
For Jayan

Cathy Aman

MAGIC NIGHT

I met a genie in a lamp.
He taught me how
to warm the damp.
He taught me how
to choose good cheese.
He taught me how to
catch a breeze.
He taught me how
to melt a shield.
He taught me how
to gaze a field.
He taught me how
to sweeten milk.
He taught me how
to spin fine silk.
He taught me about
the butterfly.
He taught me how
to never die.

I met a fairy
near the pond.
She gave to me
her magic wand.
She gave to me
a love so free.
She gave to me
a bumble bee.
She gave to me
a small shy fawn.
She gave to me
the breath of dawn.

She gave to me
a heaven of blue.
She gave to me
a kiss of dew.
She gave to me
a flute of reed.
She gave to me
the life I lead…

I met a man
by the stream
and now I live
this endless dream.…
And now I live
to have no past.
Now I live
in love a last.

Aberdeen, SD.
March 9,1971

Cathy Aman

MIDNIGHT POET

I opened my heart
    and soon it began to flow out,
       across the pages
           then from my eyes
          my nose…

'til my very core began to shake.
    The walls shattered
       letting its contents splash
          out upon the page,
           across the floor.

              Durham NH
              November 1980

MIND OF ICE

Crystal Mind
      cracked like ice
bleeding tears
      upon the snow.

New Hampshire
August 21, 1981

NEW HAMPSHIRE FIELD

Rocks, and stones
grass, and trees
ruffled hair in melodious breeze.

White birch dance
against blue sky
air of warmth sun so high.

Finches sing
blue jays call
mammoth trees with buds so small.

All are jewels
of a season new.
Winter passes spring is due.

> Durham NH
> May 3, 1980
> laying in the grass

NO SMOKING

QUEST

I was wondering
    so I went to the park
    to see if it was there.
            I crossed the tracks
                    and climbed a fence.
                    but it wasn't there.
I had a question
    so I went to the moon
    to search for the answer.
            it was dark and
                    took a long time.
                    but the moon didn't know.
I tried to decide
    so I climbed a mountain
    to ask advice.
            I struggled hard
                    to reach the top.
                    but the mountain couldn't help.
I had doubts
    so I went to the sea
    for assurance.
            the waves were rough
            and the spray cold.
                    but the sea kept it's secret.
I needed understanding
    so I went to the people
    they wore painted smiles,
            spoke tinseled words,
                    and sweet greetings
                    but they didn't understand.

                        Aberdeen, SD.
                        April 1971

Cathy Aman

REFUGEE

Limited, listless
      my eyes squelch up.
         tears fall in salty beads
            over the brims.

Painted heart.
      I wore a white mask
         so you wouldn't be afraid
            to come in.

Reach out now
      I am but a wasteland,
         a city gutted
            by war.

But touch me
      I am warm as desert sand
         and shed my tears
            for you.

Durham, NH
November 30,1980

REPENTANCE

Tears fall upon my cheeks
    like icy cycles from a winter's roof

Tears; a sign of thawing
    this ice hardened heart.

Tears evaporate
    rising into radiant clouds of love.

Tears; the showering rain
    give rise to dormant seeds of cosmic spring..

New York City
1977

Cathy Aman

ROOTS

Our roots,
our roots,
God did sow.
So from our roots,
we have to grow.

It's those roots
that told me
what to be.
So I grow
as this kind of tree.

And those roots
from which
I grow, sometimes
make me
very slow.

I looked up
and said, "Lord God
I am NOT a tree,
but a man (woman)
so must be Free!"

Boston, Huntington Ave. 1993

SIRVAVIGADAS*

His arms are the ones I want
    wrapped around me.

He held me once, me, I remember the
    comfort but cannot recall the touch.

We made love, but I can't
    recall our body's meeting.

He split open my soul,
    and when he walked away.

My anxiety fled, but so did my thought
    can I care again?

No pain, but what an odd emptiness.
    a part of me here, a part there.

Time passes, wasted, settling
    into nothing

Once I wanted to kill.
    but even my rage has escaped me.

Cathy Aman

Am I dying, or finding
    some new kind of peace?

No matter.. Even peace is wasted
    if not shared..

* Hungarian-English term for weeping - feasting.

Waltham, MA December 1992

SPRING SNOW

Gray sky
    dusk
a rumble if thunder.

Large flakes of
    spring snow
tenderness meets tenderness,

as magnolias
    are covered
in a laced veil of white.

Cathy Aman

THE MOON

Looking out
I saw
the moon.

This August moon.
A pendant,
silvery coin.

Shinning out
against
the velvet sky.

Through the space
of darkness
I felt a quiver within.

Stirred by the
breathless silence
of this immobile beauty.

Berry Town, New York International
Leadership Seminars 1980's

TRAVELER

The sun sets,
but in another place,
    it rises,
bringing the dawn
    of a new day.

    As the veil
of darkness lifts
    the color of
life is revealed.
    And the day is new.

    Sunrise
brings a glow,
    a melted golden
warmth that pores out
    along the horizon.

Durham, NH
Summer 1980

Cathy Aman

UNDER THE NIGHT

She sat out under the
    night sky.
The whole world seemed
    to stand still.

Laced white clouds
    hung like a doily
over her quiet
    upturned face.

She didn't grumble
    at the drifting white flakes
but imagined them a veil
    and she the bride.

Occasional stars
    like diamond studs
poked out through
    the blackened sky.

I listened for
    her absent song
and in the silence
    heard music..

URBAN WALK

Old borrower
    A long afternoon of begging
Feet aching
    Pounding bones on pavement
Now sinking down
    onto a stone ledge.

Dirty fingers
    molded like old clay
around a paper covered can.
    Cuff vanishing,
worn as his spirit into a fray.

Exhausted in his labors.
    A look of defeat
Tomorrow awaits another day
    of laboring. Working
at the only job he knows.

           New York City

YOU

One word,
   a portrait
hung in the gallery
    of my heart.

SONGS

Cathy Aman

A NEW DAY HAS BEGUN

I awoke one morning
to the falling of the rain
I saw a world before me
of misery and pain.

I looked beyond the clouds,
saw the peering of the sun,
although the sky was darkened,
a new day had begun.

A new day
    has begun
        for everyone!.

There's a certain freshness
that follows morning rain.
Life blooms all around us.
New hope is regained.

A rainbow stands before us.
The promise has come true.
Our hearts are reawakened
reaching out to you.

A new day
    has begun
        for everyone!

Horizons clear at midday.
The sun is shining high.
The path I walk is open.
My heart finds wings to fly.
I often stop to question

and wonder in my mind,
why this light of truth
was so difficult to find.

A new day
    has begun
       for everyone!

Now I have found a treasure
that gold cannot replace.
Like a flawless jewel
I saw his shining face.

When I look at the river,
our destiny is clear.
All men will be brothers
and all the world will hear.

A new day
    has begun
       for everyone!

A new day
    has begun
       for everyone!

A new age is upon us.
God's love has claimed the earth.
As we join in oneness
the world will find rebirth.

A new day
    has begun
       for everyone!

Up State New York

Cathy Aman

A SONG THAT WAITS TO BE SUNG

You are a song
that waits to be sung,
a river deep
that waits to be swum.

Like an evening
that waits for a star
in the dark moment
you feel so far

I feel the
North wind
blowing straight
through my heart.

But you are a hope
like an evening breeze
that comforts the sun
as it sinks past the trees.

You fill my mind
with whispers and fire
kindle my strength
beyond all desire.

Reaching high
higher…
to what life can be
I am free.

1984

CARRY LOVE TO THE WORLD

What do you see when you look at me?
Where do you go when you want to know?
And how do you feel when you know that it's real?

Carry love carry love carry love to the world.

What is the beach when there's no longer a sea?
Where's the song of a heart never sung?
And how do you feel when your soul's really ripe?

Carry love carry love carry love to the world

Some live in anger.
Another lives in strife.
One girl is lonely. Another a wife

Carry love carry love carry love to the world

Bring someone silence.
Another new love.
Someone a dog , horse, or a dove.

Carry love carry love carry love to the world.

Cathy Aman

COME AND SING WITH ME

Come and sing with me.
Let your heart flow,
free and easily
like the breezes the blow.

    Over mountains high
    and valleys low.
    Share your heart cause I want to know.

Know who you are
where you're coming from.
Where you have been
where you're going to.

    Open wide.
    Let me see inside
    the heart that's really you.

Heart that glows throughout
the darkest night
Dance in mystery as
the Northern lights.

    Reveal yourself
    and let me share
    how much I really care.

Let us sing a song
in purest heart
Love as crystals clear
we'll never part.

Prismed rainbows
on the wall.
We'll be one embracing all.

Durham, NH
June 21, 1980
Munehiro's Birthday

Cathy Aman

COME TO THE MOUNTAIN

Come onto my mountain.
Come sit beside my stream.
Come breath my fragrant air now
and live inside my dream.

I dream of lands of beauty
of an everlasting sun.
I dream of hearts of loving
when we and God are one.

I hope to make this dream live
even with my sweat and tears.
To see it blooming fully
where all are free from fears.

Come take my hand walk slowly.
Come leave your grief behind.
I know you've been so lonely.
Now free that ancient mind.

I hope to make this dream live,
stay alive within my heart.
To see it blooming fully
a dream of which we are all part.

We'll live a life of loving
where our giving finds no bounds.
And there our true selves,
in full bloom will be found.

DO YOU KNOW ME?

Hey, you'll never know my heart
while you run and play in the grass.
Cause though you see me standing here
you're only looking through glass.

Where do you go in winter?
Do you run and look for the sea?
Where do you go when summer comes?
Will you be looking for me?

I'm not made of steel
and I'm not made of gold.
But what's inside you've never heard,
'cause my story's never been told .

Yes, you saw me smiling
because I hid all of my tears.
How could you know
what I've seen in my traveling years.

You stayed at home
warm and secure.
In your comfort you couldn't hear,
the human cries that I heard so clear.

Now caught in today.
No eyes for past or tomorrow.
But the world rolls on
with her history of heart break and sorrow.

You would drown in the river
of tears that were cried
by people with dreams,
who failed when they tried

1982

FACE OF A STAR

I saw your face
shine out that night,
it looked like
a star in the night.

Shining like silver
diamonds and gold.
I said to myself,
it's a treasure I never can hold.

Oh, oh face of a star,
shining out in the night.
Oh, oh face of the star,
reflecting Heaven's light.

You spoke in a whisper,
soft as a breeze
about
your love for me.

My words fell like darkness
onto the night
against the glow
of our light.

Oh, oh face of the star,
shining out in the night.
Oh, oh face of the star,
reflecting heaven's light.

Cathy Aman

But you flowed like water
purer than snow
you said you wanted me
for your own.

So I picked up my coat
straightened my hair
and said
"I'm ready to go".

Oh, oh face of the star,
shining out in the night.
Oh, oh face of the star,
reflecting heavens light.

You took me to water
that quivered with life
and asked if
I knew how to swim.

I saw a reflection.
Her eyes were like mine
but strangely enough,
her heart was filled to the brim.

Oh, oh face of the star,
shining out in the night.
Oh, oh face of the star,
reflecting heaven's light.

You held my hand.
We stood on the bank.
You told me to
get in.

I looked into your eyes
turned and I dove
and found that
I too could win.

Now I have the face of a star
shining out in the night.
I have the face of the star
reflecting Heaven's light.

Winter 1982
Dover, NH

GIFT

May I give you
a piece of the night?
A piece of the
star lit sky?

Or may I give you
the breath of the wind
that silently
passes by?

May I give you
a touch of the land
that sleeps with
the memory of spring?

Or may I give you
one true love,
a kiss,
and a golden ring?

HOLD ON TO YOUR LOVE

They can say you gotta
stand on your own.
And that's OK
'cause in fact we're all alone.

But hold on
hold on
hold on to your love!

So I don't need
no good reason
to stay by your side
It's just love and nothin' to hide.

Hold on
hold on
hold on to your love!

Some body says
they'll make you a deal
call it "Love"
and try to say that it's real.

But hold on
hold on
hold on to your love!

Cathy Aman

HOLD ON

Just a little while longer
'til you're gonna see the sun.

Always after darkness comes the morning,
A warm and glorious embrace.

Oh don't run away from the dawning.
You've already waited so long.

Hold on with all of your longing.
In the day you'll again feel strong.

1982

I MISS YOU IN THE MORNING

I miss you in the morning
when the sun begins to rise.
And wish that I were near you
so I could look into your eyes.

That you were here beside me
your body close to mine.
That we could share the morning
as the sun begins to shine.

You bring me such comfort.
And you are so sincere.
I love you and I need you.
I'm missing you my dear.

But I'm listening to the radio
instead of to your voice
I hear songs of love and words of war
and wish I had a choice.

You'd be here beside me
and no one would object.
Cause you're the kind of guy
that they all will respect.

I will hold you near
your ear upon my heart
I'll touch you so tender
as we make a new start.

Cathy Aman

We'll enjoy the days before us
and the days ahead
build dreams and promises
from our wedding bed.

I miss you in the morning
when the sun begins to rise.
And wish that I were near you
so I could look into your eyes.

Winter 1990

I NEVER LET YOU KNOW

I never let you know my heart,
how it was flown.
I never let you know my life
which way it was go'n.

But now I have come to see,
and I want to make you free.
I want to put your thoughts at ease,
and make your heart feel breezy.

I only gave you tribulation.
Now I'll give you inspiration.
I never gave you peace of mind,
but now you're going to find…

The season's here to bloom
and I'm finding so much room
for loving you.
I'm going to see it through.

1981

Cathy Aman

I'LL LOVE YOU AGAIN AND AGAIN

My heart burns true
in my love for you

I can't hold back
my desire

I want to fly
above the silvery sky

Where my love will never die
today, tonight, or tomorrow.

There'll be no lies
no thieving disguise

For my love is strong
I'll write you a brand new song.

So come tonight
or take the next flight

Oh I know your soul
You'll be here tomorrow.

We'll sing and we'll write
make love through the night.

I'll love you again and again (round: again and again)
I'll love you today and tomorrow (again and again).

I'll love you again and again
that life will never end.

I'll love you today (again and again)
I'll love you tonight (again and again and again and again)
and I'll love you again tomorrow.

1998

Cathy Aman

I'LL MISS YOU

Well, we'll miss you
when you've gone away
And will listen to
what you've got to say.

Say it now
while you're here!
Say it loud.
Say it clear.

The time
won't be long.
You'll go.
I know you're strong.

You may not
know where I've been
Or seen what
I have seen.

But it's pure
and it's true
makes me feel
that I'll always love you.

I'LL NEVER LEAVE YOU

Oh I'll never leave you.
I'll never go home.
I'll stay by your side.
Never leave you alone.

Let love rule your heart.
Let love rule your soul.
In love we begin to grow.

No I'll never deceive you.
Never break your heart.
Please know that I love you
and don't want to part.

For I want to be with you.
Always there by your side.
Yes you are my life dear.
You are my pride.

Let love rule your heart.
Let love rule your soul.
In love we begin to grow.

Let us live our lives happy.
Let us live our lives strong.
Let us live for each other.
For our life's not too long.

Cathy Aman

I'll always be with you.
My heart ever true
as we climb through the valleys,
and to Heaven when we're through.

Let love rule your heart.
Let love rule your soul.
In love we begin to grow.

JUSTICE

Oh Justice,
like a mountain against the sky
never leave my side
rolling like the sea
flow into my soul.

Oh Justice,
stand strong as waves
that slap their salty tears
into the rocky shore and
drawn back to the depths of the oceans floor.

Oh Justice,
you have a face
stern as one carved of stone
yet when in your place
lie softer than new winter snow.

Oh Justice,
I'll never let go
but stand as one crying out your name and
pray for your face to show
as I wonder if I'm to blame for the injustice that remains.

Oh Justice,
your answer won't be in vain
for the world of those in shattered heart ache
long to end their pain.
In hope that justice will rise again.

Oh Justice,
Justice,
Oh Justice
In your presence,
the world won't die in shame.

Cathy Aman

LOVE ABIDES

They were her parents.
She was their girl.
They were her gods.
She was their world.

Dreams of tomorrow
upon the great plains.
Shadow of yesteryear
only remains.

A great river bends
and a river divides.
Miles between us
but love still abides.

Tears gathered at mid-night
to dance on the dew.
Don't cry now Mama.
Your little girl grew.

Hungered for meaning
in the wells of her mind.
Searching for something
she couldn't define.

Oh Mama an Papa
like gold your hearts gleam.
Eternal long river
fed by two streams.

Durham, NH
Summer 1980
Song for parents Anniversary

LOVE IS WAITING

So many miles have passed us by.
So many tears we all have cried.
Now it is time to see the sun.
Open your hearts now everyone!

Love is waiting!
Love is waiting!
Love is there.

Too many yesterdays still hang on.
Too many days without a song.
Let your sorrows say good-bye
cause I know if you will try,

Love is waiting!
Love is waiting!
Love is here!

So you've been hurt and don't want to let go
and you think that it won't show.
You want to live free to see tomorrow
but can't cause you're holding sorrow.

Love is waiting!
Love is waiting!
Love is here!

Cathy Aman

OLD WOMAN

Old woman sad and alone
what will you do now?
Where will you go?

Your prime years
have passed now.
The sun is getting low.

Your young years
are memories that
fade in dimmed light.

Old woman,
are you lonely tonight?

Old woman you dream like a girl.
Dance in the moonlight
as leaves blow, and swirl.

Old woman,
are you lonely tonight?

Your eyes still
hold a sparkle
in the soft candle light .

You're one who
loved me when
I couldn't hold my own.

Old woman,
may you never feel alone.

Now you stand
in the winter
of your life.

Old woman,
may your days be free of strife.

Old woman,
are you lonely tonight?

Old woman,
may your days be free of strife.

Cathy Aman

ON-CORE

Sing a song for the On-Core.
We're the hope that's coming true.

We'll fight the battle
with our tears, sweat, and blood
we're asking you to come too.

Sing a song for the On-Core.
We'll stand bold in face of destiny.

Our brothers have been suffering
for far too long.
Let's unite to set them free.

Sing a song with the On-Core.
Let's build the world of our ideals.

Lift our crumbling race
to shine again.
Sacrifice yourself to make it true.

Sing a song with the On-Core.
Facing rejection every step we take.

We'll persevere with love
and stand up proud
reflecting the ideal world we'll make.

Durham, NH

PENDULUM

As a pendulum swings
and time passes by
many thoughts through my mind fly.

As the pendulum swings
and time passes by
I wonder when this world will fly
like a kite above the clouds.

As my thoughts like a kite
drift through the sky
my tears fall so lonely the whole while I cry.

As my thoughts like a kite
drift through the sky
I wonder when this world will fly
like a kite above the clouds

As the desert is heated
by rays of the sun
my love must warm another sad one.

As the desert is heated
by rays of the sun
I know many are broken and searching for one
to let them dance as the sea.

So dance as the waves
set your soul free
you must decide what your life will be.

So dance as the waves
set your soul free

what you make of your life is what it will be
don't let time pass you by.

Durham ,NH
June 14, 1980

PENNY WISE

Penny wise, and heart foolish
standing here in the snow.

Penny wise, and heart foolish
when will you know?

That you're penny wise, and heart foolish
your heart as cold as ice and snow.

Oh penny wise, and heart foolish
why can't you let your feelings show?

Your mind a cell a vacant prison.
Your mind a witches spell.

Penny wise, and heart foolish
in a world of living hell.

Penny wise, and heart foolish
walk the streets of winter's night.

Loneliness has found its cavern.
When will you see the light ?

Penny wise, and heart foolish
your gloom begins to show.

Look and see the truth now.
You've no place left to go.

Penny wise, and heart foolish
love won't hurt you know.

Cathy Aman

Standing in the winter snow
under a lone street lamp.

Wondering where you will go
where you can call your home.

Penny wise, and heart foolish
you've no place left to go.

RAIN

I heard water falling.
It was from the rain.
As I listened to the water
you were the refrain.

Your love is like spring music
that falls down from above.
The song sounds ever new
for your song is of our love.

You sang to me at midnight
when the world turned out its light.
But in the flow of your sweet music
I danced in shadowed light.

La la la la la la
la la la la laa
la la la la la
al la la la la laa

Your love is like spring music
that falls down from above.
The song sounds ever new
because you sing of our love.

Cathy Aman

RIVERS THAT RUN TO THE SEA

Just say what you need .
Just say that you care.
Just call me
and I will be there.

There are rivers
that run to the sea.
There are rivers that
run into rivers.
and rivers that run to the sea.

Just say what you need.
Just say that you care.
Just call me
and I will be there.

There are moments
in each of our hearts
when we long to be free,
just like rivers,
like rivers that run to the sea.

Just say what you need.
Just say that you care.
Call me
and I will be there.

Like a river,
like a river
Just like a river,
like a river
that runs to the sea.

SOUTH DAKOTA MEMORY

Oh I can't wait for winter, I can't wait for snow
I just can't wait for the harsh winds to blow.

> I see the flat lands lie open wide
> Barren old prairies' with no place to hide
> Clouds ride in space of unlimited blue
> And set with the sun when the long day is through

Oh I can't wait for winter, I can't wait for snow
I just can't wait for the harsh winds to blow.

> Yes I am a girl who longs for the land
> For corn fields sown by an old farmer's hand
> To stand with the cattle beneath the grand sky
> Where no ears are needed to hear God's reply

Oh I can't wait for winter, I can't wait for snow
I just can't wait for the harsh winds to blow.

> I ache for that barren expanse in my view
> The vision of infinite grasped only by few
> To hear the rain dash in a cooled summer night
> Or blizzard winds howl as the world's painted white.

Oh I can't wait for winter, I can't wait for snow
I just can't wait for those harsh winds to blow.

Durham, NH
November 30, 1980

Cathy Aman

STAR IN THE NIGHT

Two young boys sat alone at night
whistling songs under star light.

Sheep there in the pasture lay
waiting for the new born day.

Angles there by the star did sing
proclaiming, "We've come to announce a king."

Come and bring all that you are!
This was the message that came with the star.

Hail, hail! I see the light
A star, a star especially bright!

Hail! It shines so bright
that it fades the darkness of the night.

"Angels came proclaiming this star!"
was the murmur of wise men with gifts, from afar.

Hail! Hail! I see a light!
A star, a star! especially bright!

The birth of a child in a stable, on hay
reigns as King of love even today.

Hail! Hail! I see a light!
The light of a star especially bright.

A Christmas Carol
1995

TO 10TH INTERNATIONAL LEADERSHIP
SEMINAR PARTICIPANTS

Well you've been fill'n in some spaces
and you're tell'n me of places
places I have never seen before.

We've spent time together
seen sights in rainy weather
Now too soon we'll say good-bye.

But you'll be on my mind
cause a friend like you
is very hard to find.

And though we'll be apart
I hope our times will
never leave my heart.

You know this time will pass by
and I can't tell you
that I won't cry.

But hear my hope and prayer for you
for only you can
make it true.

Come give all the heart
and soul you have, let's
build a world of love.

1982

Cathy Aman

WILL YOU GO WITH ME?

I want to know if you'll go with me
I want to know if you'll go with me
Go to the mountains
Go to the sea

I want to know if you will go with me

Go to the ocean
Onto the sand
Through the cold water
In bold waves stand

I want to know if you will go with me

Climb to the mountains
Far from the sea
Into the blue sky
Over the trees

I want to know if you will go with me

Into the city
Tossed in the storm
Lonely ones crying
Old ones forlorn

I want to know, I want to know

I want to know if you will go with me

Into a dead world
Yearning for life
Hungered for meaning
Through the long night

I want to know, I want to know
I want to know if you will go…
I want to know if you will go with me.

1980

Cathy Aman

WITHOUT YOU

It's just all these days without you
Just all these hours alone
Just all these nights of loneliness
That makes me feel that I'm without a home

Oh, yes I love you
oh, oh I love you.

I just want to be by your side
Oh I didn't want to have to hide
I wanna share the love in my heart
And wish that we weren't apart

Oh, yes I love you
oh, oh I love you.

I saw with you on my side
there's so much love I've had to hide
All these hopes and dreams inside of me
I want to live out with you in reality.

Oh, yes I love you
oh, oh I love you.

To know that you're thinking of me
and that you're feeling lonely too
some how through these drawn out days
I feel we'll make it through.

Oh, yes I love you
oh, oh I love you
mmm mmm I love you
ya ya you know I love you.

YOU WILL BE MADE NEW

Please give out your heart.
You must be stronger.
We can't go on living only
in the night any longer.

Don't draw the curtains
to a day that's just begun.
Open up your mind and heart
to the glory of the bright new morning sun.

For a new day
a new day
a new day has begun
a la la la la la la la.

Don't close your eyes
to a view that's just appearing.
Don't be afraid for the darkness of this
fog will soon be clearing.

For a new day
a new day
A new day has begun
A la la la la la la la

You can hold that vision,
that seed to your ideal.
Go do it. It's growing fragrance is
the blooming of a cherished dream made real.

Cathy Aman

For a new day
a new day
A new day has begun
A la la la la la la la

I didn't know that
your loneliness was true.
But now's the time for joy
your life will be made new.

A new day
a new day
A new day has begun
A la la la la la la la

You can hold that vision
that seed to your ideal
go do it, it's growing fragrance is
the blooming if a cherished dream made real.

I didn't know that
your loneliness was true
but now's the time for joy
your life will be made new.

A new day
a new day
A new day has begun

A la la la la la la la

YOU'RE THE ONLY ONE

Well there's never gonna be
another one like you.
There's never been one before.
Don't mind if you're the one that I adore.

I was walking through dark
and shadowed places
surrounded by sad
and mournful faces.

They cried out for help
but I had nothing to give.
Cause I was holding on
just try'n to live .

Well, now there's you
and I believe
that you're the one
I'll never deceive.

You see right through
to the core of my heart.
Make me feel OK
when I don't know how to start.

We'll live a life of loving
where our giving finds no bounds.
And there our true selves
will in full bloom be found.

About the Author

Cathy Aman grew up in the plains of South Dakota. Both of her parents were educators. She is the second of four children. The beauty of the land and skies around her inspired her to begin painting and writing poems about them when she was 6 years old. Though she came from a mixed religious family, she was raised Catholic and had a strong love of Christ. At age 16, she moved from her parents' home to Minneapolis where she soon separated from the 70s Dinky Town crowd into a yoga community. Her spiritual journey continued in its intensity for 15 years exposing her to practices of both eastern and western philosophies, Jewish and Christian mysticism. This journey was physical as well. She traveled through 46 of the United States and international communities within the United States. She performed as a dancer with the International Folk Ballet for 3 years in New York City and on two U.S. tours. She lived in metropolitan Philadelphia, New York, San Diego, Minneapolis and Boston. She has given many public lectures on various topics and is a graduate of the University of New Hampshire where she did graduate level courses in poetry writing with poetess Mekeel McBride. She is an admirer of the works of contemporary poet, Professor Charles Simac.

Cathy is a Christian, artist, speaker, administrator, has experience as a health practicioner and is the mother of one daughter, Megan. Though a very intense part of her journey has ended, she feels that the whole of life with it's difficulties and pleasures can teach us to know God's love and be more compassionate toward our fellow human beings.